A Beginners Guide

to Keto Diet Recipes

Cookbook with Keto Recipes for beginners

and lazy people.

Including Yummy Recipes to Reset Your

Body

William King

Table of Contents

This declaration is deemed fair and valid by both the American Bar Association and the Committee of Publishers Association and is legally binding throughout the United States.

Furthermore, the transmission, duplication, or reproduction of any of the following work including specific information will be considered an illegal act irrespective of if it is done electronically or in print. This extends to creating a secondary or tertiary copy of the work or a recorded copy and is only allowed with the express written consent from the Publisher. All additional right reserved.

The information in the following pages is broadly considered a truthful and accurate account of facts and as such, any inattention, use, or misuse of the information in question by the reader will render any resulting actions solely under their purview. There are no scenarios in which the publisher or the original author of this work can be in any fashion deemed liable for any hardship or damages that may befall them after undertaking information described herein. Additionally, the information in the following pages is intended only for informational purposes and should thus be thought of as universal. As befitting its nature, it is presented without assurance regarding its prolonged validity or interim quality.

Trademarks that are mentioned are done without written consent and can in no way be considered an endorsement from the trademark holder.

INTRODUCTION

So the Ketogenic Diet is all about reducing the amount of carbohydrates you eat. Does this mean you won't get the kind of energy you need for the day? Of course not! It only means that now, your body has to find other possible sources of energy. Do you know where they will be getting that energy?

Even before we talk about how to do keto – it's important to first consider why this particular diet works. What actually happens to your body to make you lose weight?

As you probably know, the body uses food as an energy source. Everything you eat is turned into energy, so that you can get up and do whatever you need to accomplish for the day. The main energy source is sugar so what happens is that you eat something, the body breaks it down into sugar, and the sugar is processed into energy. Typically, the "sugar" is taken directly from the food you eat so if you eat just the right amount of food, then your body is fueled for the whole day. If you eat too much, then the sugar is stored in your body – hence the accumulation of fat.

But what happens if you eat less food? This is where the Ketogenic Diet comes in. You see, the process of creating sugar from food is usually faster if the food happens to be rich in carbohydrates. Bread, rice, grain, pasta – all of these are carbohydrates and they're the easiest food types to turn into energy.

So here's the situation – you are eating less carbohydrates every day. To keep you energetic, the body breaks down the stored fat and turns them into molecules called ketone bodies. The process of turning the fat into ketone bodies is called "Ketosis" and obviously – this is where the name of the Ketogenic Diet comes from. The ketone bodies take the place of glucose in keeping you energetic. As long as you keep your carbohydrates reduced, the body will keep getting its energy from your body fat.

The Ketogenic Diet is often praised for its simplicity and when you look at it properly, the process is really straightforward. The Science behind the effectivity of the diet is also well-documented, and has been proven multiple times by different medical fields. For example, an article on Diet Review by Harvard provided a lengthy discussion on how the Ketogenic Diet works and why it is so effective for those who choose to use this diet.

But Fat Is the Enemy...Or Is It?

No – fat is NOT the enemy. Unfortunately, years of bad science told us that fat is something you have to avoid – but it's actually a very helpful thing for weight loss! Even before we move forward with this book, we'll have to discuss exactly what "healthy fats" are, and why they're actually the good guys. To do this, we need to make a distinction between the different kinds of fat. You've probably heard of them before and it is a little bit confusing at first. We'll try to go through them as simply as possible: Saturated fat. This is the kind you want to avoid. They're also called "solid fat" because each molecule is packed with hydrogen atoms. Simply put, it's the kind of fat that can easily cause a blockage in your body. It can raise cholesterol levels and lead to heart problems or a stroke. Saturated fat is something you can find in meat, dairy products, and other processed food items. Now, you're probably wondering: isn't the Ketogenic Diet packed with saturated fat? The answer is: not necessarily. You'll find later in the recipes given that the Ketogenic Diet promotes primarily unsaturated fat or healthy fat. While there are definitely many meat recipes in the list, most of these recipes contain healthy fat sources. Unsaturated Fat. These are the ones dubbed as healthy fat. They're the kind of fat you find in avocado, nuts, and other ingredients you usually find in Keto-friendly recipes. They're known to lower blood cholesterol and actually come in two types: polyunsaturated and monounsaturated. Both are good for your body but the benefits slightly vary, depending on what you're consuming.

Asian Chicken with Fresh Lime-Peanut Sauce

Preparation Time: 1 HOUR AND 30 MINUTES

Cooking Time: 40 MINUTES

Servings: 6

Ingredients

- 1 tbsp. wheat-free soy sauce

- 1 tbsp. sugar-free fish sauce

- 1 tbsp. lime juice

- 1 tsp coriander

- 1 tsp garlic, minced

- 1 tsp ginger, minced

- 1 tbsp. olive oil

- 1 tbsp. rice wine vinegar

- 1 tsp cayenne pepper

- 1 tbsp. erythritol

- 6 chicken thighs

- **Sauce:**

- ½ cup peanut butter

- 1 tsp garlic, minced

- 1 tbsp. lime juice

- 2 tbsp. water

- 1 tsp ginger, minced

  1 tbsp. jalapeño, chopped

- 2 tbsp. rice wine vinegar

- 2 tbsp. erythritol

- 1 tbsp. fish sauce

Directions

1. Combine all of the chicken ingredients in a large Ziploc bag.

2. Seal the bag and shake to combine.

3. Refrigerate for about 1 hour.

4. Remove from the fridge about 15 minutes before cooking.

5. Preheat the grill to medium, and grill the chicken for about 7 minutes per side.

6. Meanwhile, whisk together all of the sauce ingredients in a mixing bowl.

7. Serve the chicken drizzled with peanut sauce.

Nutrition

Calories 492,

Net Carbs 3g,

Fat 36g,

Protein 35g

Chicken with Eggplant & Tomatoes

Preparation Time: 25 MINUTES

Cooking Time: 10 MINUTES

Servings: 4

Ingredients

- 2 tbsp. ghee

- 1 lb. chicken thighs

- Salt and black pepper to taste

- 2 cloves garlic, minced

- 1 (14 oz.) can whole tomatoes

- 1 eggplant, diced

- 10 fresh basil leaves, chopped + extra to garnish

Directions

1. Melt ghee in a saucepan over medium heat, season the chicken with salt and black pepper, and fry for 4 minutes on each side until golden brown. Remove the chicken onto a plate.

2. Sauté the garlic in the ghee for 2 minutes, pour in the tomatoes, and cook covered for 8 minutes. Include the eggplant and basil. Cook for 4 minutes.

3. Season the sauce with salt and black pepper, stir and add the chicken. Coat with sauce and simmer for 3 minutes.

4. Serve chicken with sauce on a bed of squash pasta garnished with basil.

Nutrition

Calories 468,

Net Carbs 2g,

Fat 39.5g,

Protein 26g

Rosemary Chicken with Avocado Sauce

Preparation Time: 22 MINUTES

Cooking Time: 30 MINUTES

Servings: 4 |

Ingredients

- 1 avocado pitted

- ½ cup mayonnaise

- 3 tbsp. ghee

- 4 chicken breasts

- Salt and black pepper to taste

- 1 cup rosemary, chopped

- ½ cup chicken broth

Directions

1. Spoon avocado, mayonnaise, and salt into a food processor and puree until a smooth

sauce is derived. Adjust the taste with salt. Pour sauce into a jar and refrigerate.

2. Melt ghee in a large skillet, season chicken with salt and black pepper, and fry for 4 minutes on each side to a golden brown. Remove chicken to a plate.

3. Pour the broth in the same skillet and add the cilantro. Bring to simmer covered for 3 minutes and add the chicken. Cover, and cook on low heat for 5 minutes until the liquid has reduced and chicken is fragrant.

4. Dish chicken only into serving plates and spoon the mayo-avocado sauce over.

5. Serve warm with buttered green beans and baby carrots.

Nutrition Calories 398, Net Carbs 4g, Fat 32g,

Protein 24g

Tasty Chicken with Brussel Sprouts

Preparation Time: 120 MINUTES

Cooking Time: 40 MINUTES

Servings: 8

Ingredients

- 5 pounds whole chicken

- 1 bunch oregano

- 1 bunch thyme

- 1 tbsp. marjoram

- 1 tbsp. parsley

- 1 tbsp. olive oil

- 2 pounds Brussel sprouts

- 1 lemon

- 4 tbsp. butter

Directions

1. Preheat your oven to 450 F.

2. Stuff the chicken with oregano, thyme, and lemon.

3. Make sure the wings are tucked over and behind.

4. Roast for 15 minutes. Reduce the heat to 325 F, and cook for 40 minutes.

5. Spread the butter over the chicken and sprinkle parsley and marjoram.

6. Add the Brussel sprouts. Return to oven and bake for 40 more minutes.

7. Let sit for 10 minutes before carving.

Nutrition Calories 430, Net Carbs 5g, Fat 32g,

Protein 30g

SIDE DISHES

Chili Cauliflower Mix

Preparation Time: 10 minutes

Cooking Time: 35 minutes

Servings: 4

Ingredients:

- 2 tablespoons sweet chili sauce

- 3 tablespoons olive oil

- 3 garlic cloves, minced

- Juice of 1 lime

- 1 cauliflower head, florets separated

- 1 teaspoon cilantro, chopped

- A pinch of salt and black pepper

Directions:

1. In a bowl, the chili sauce with the oil, garlic, lime juice, salt, pepper, cilantro and the cauliflower, toss well, spread on a lined baking sheet, introduce in the oven and cook at 425 degrees F for 35 minutes.

2. Divide the cauliflower between plates and serve as a side dish.

Nutrition:

Calories: 271

Fat: 4

Fiber: 7,

Carbohydrates: 11

Protein: 7

Mozzarella Brussels Sprouts
Preparation Time: 10 minutes

Cooking Time: 30 minutes

Servings: 6

Ingredients:

- 2 tablespoons olive oil

- 2 pounds Brussels sprouts

- 2 garlic cloves, minced

- 1 teaspoon thyme, chopped

- A pinch of salt and black pepper

- 1 cup mozzarella, shredded

- ¼ cup parmesan, grated

- 1 tablespoon parsley, chopped

Directions:

1. Put some water in a pot, bring to a boil over medium-high heat, add sprouts, cook them for 10 minutes, transfer them to a bowl filled with ice water, cool them down and drain them well.

2. In a bowl, combine the Brussels sprouts with salt, pepper, oil, garlic and thyme, toss and smash them a bit.

3. Spread smashed Brussels sprouts on a lined baking sheet, sprinkle mozzarella and parmesan on top, introduce in the oven and bake them at 425 degrees F for 20 minutes.

4. Sprinkle parsley on top, divide between plates and serve as a side dish.

Nutrition:

Calories: 288

Fat: 4 Fiber: 6

Carbohydrates: 13

Protein: 6

Mozzarella Broccoli Mix

Preparation Time: 10 minutes

Cooking Time: 15 minutes

Servings: 4

Ingredients:

- 2 tablespoons olive oil
- 1 broccoli head, florets separated
- 2 garlic cloves, minced
- ½ cup mozzarella, shredded
- ¼ cup parmesan, grated
- ½ cup coconut cream
- 1 tablespoon parsley, chopped

Directions:

1. Heat up a pan with the oil over medium-high heat add broccoli, salt, pepper and garlic, stir and cook for 6 minutes.

2. Add parmesan, mozzarella and cream, toss, introduce the pan in the oven and cook at 375 degrees F for 10 minutes.

3. Add parsley, toss, divide between plates and serve as a side dish.

Nutrition:

Calories: 261
Fat: 4

Fiber: 4

Carbohydrates: 13

Protein: 8

Parsley Bacon Brussels Sprouts

Preparation Time: 10 minutes

Cooking Time: 20 minutes

Servings: 6

Ingredients:

- 1-pound Brussels sprouts, halved
- A pinch of salt and black pepper
- 7 bacon slices, chopped
- 1 yellow onion, chopped
- 2 tablespoons stevia
- 2 tablespoons olive oil
- 1 tablespoon parsley, chopped
- 2 teaspoons sweet paprika

Directions:

1. Heat up a pan with the oil over medium-high heat, add the onion, stir and sauté for 4-5 minutes.

2. Add the bacon, stir and cook for 3 minutes more.

3. Add the sprouts, salt, pepper, stevia, paprika and parsley, toss, cook for 10 minutes more, divide between plates and serve as a side dish.

Nutrition:

Calories: 261

Fat: 4

Fiber: 8

Carbohydrates: 12

Protein: 8

Mediterranean Side Salad

Preparation Time: 10 minutes

Cooking Time: 0 minutes

Servings: 4

Ingredients:

- 1-pint cherry tomatoes, halved

- 1 cup kalamata olives, pitted and sliced

- 1 cucumber, sliced

- ½ red onion, sliced

- 1 cup feta cheese, crumbled

- Juice of ½ lemon

- 2 tablespoons red vinegar

- A pinch of salt and black pepper

- 1 teaspoon oregano, dried

- ¼ cup olive oil

Directions:

1. In a salad bowl, combine the tomatoes with the olives, cucumber and onion.

2. In a separate bowl, combine the lemon juice with the vinegar, salt, pepper, oregano and oil and whisk well.

3. Pour this over your salad, toss, sprinkle cheese at the end and serve as a side dish.

Nutrition:

Calories: 200 Fat: 3

Fiber: 6

Carbohydrates: 12

Protein: 8

Mozzarella and Artichoke Mix

Preparation Time: 10 minutes

Cooking Time: 10 minutes

Servings: 4

Ingredients:

- 14 ounces canned artichoke hearts, drained
- A pinch of salt and black pepper
- 2 cups baby spinach
- 2 tablespoons parsley, chopped
- 1 cup mozzarella, shredded
- Juice of 1 lemon
- 1 and ¾ cup coconut milk
- ½ cup chicken stock
- 2 garlic cloves, minced
- 3 tablespoons ghee, melted

- A pinch of red pepper flakes

Directions:

1. Heat up a pan with the ghee over medium-high heat, add the garlic, stir and cook for 2 minutes.

2. Add lemon juice, coconut milk, stock, artichokes, salt and pepper, stir and cook for 5 minutes.

3. Add spinach, pepper flakes and mozzarella, toss, cook for 3 minutes more, and divide between plates, sprinkle parsley on top and serve as a side dish.

Nutrition:

Calories: 277 Fat: 3 Fiber: 6 Carbohydrates: 12

Protein: 8

Roasted Brussels Sprouts

Preparation Time: 10 minutes

Cooking Time: 25 minutes

Servings: 4

Ingredients:

- 1-pound Brussels sprouts, halved

- 2 tablespoons olive oil

- A pinch of salt and black pepper

Directions:

1. Spread the sprouts on a lined baking sheet, add the oil, salt and pepper, toss, introduce in the oven and bake at 425 degrees F for 25 minutes.

2. Divide between plates and serve as a side dish.

Nutrition:

Calories: 200

Fat: 2 Fiber: 6

Carbohydrates: 11

Protein: 8

Rosemary Veggie Mix

Preparation Time: 10 minutes

Cooking Time: 20 minutes

Servings: 4

Ingredients:

- 1-pound Brussels sprouts, halved

- 2 tablespoons olive oil

- 1 teaspoon rosemary, chopped

- 1 tablespoon balsamic vinegar

- 1 teaspoon thyme, chopped

- ½ cup cranberries, dried

Directions:

1. Spread the sprouts on a lined baking sheet, add rosemary, vinegar, oil and thyme, toss, introduce in the oven and cook at 400 degrees F for 20 minutes.

2. Divide between plates, sprinkle cranberries on top and serve as a side dish.

Nutrition:

Calories: 199

Fat: 3 Fiber: 5

Carbohydrates: 12

Protein: 7

Citric Cauliflower Rice

Preparation Time: 10 minutes

Cooking Time: 15 minutes

Servings: 4

Ingredients:

- 1 tablespoon ghee, melted

- Juice of 2 limes

- A pinch of salt and black pepper

- 1 cup cauliflower rice

- 1 and ½ cups veggie stock

- 1 tablespoon cilantro, chopped

Directions:

1. Heat up a pan with the ghee over medium-high heat, add the cauliflower rice, stir and cook for 5 minutes.

2. Add lime juice, salt, pepper and stock, stir, bring to a simmer and cook for 10 minutes.

3. Add cilantro, toss, divide between plates and serve as a side dish.

Nutrition:

Calories: 200

Fat: 3

Fiber: 6

Carbohydrates: 9

Protein: 6

Zoodles Side Dish

Preparation Time: 10 minutes

Cooking Time: 0 minutes

Servings: 4

Ingredients:

- 4 zucchinis, cut with a spiralizer

- 2 tablespoons olive oil

- A pinch of salt and black pepper

- 1 cup mozzarella, shredded

- 2 cups cherry tomatoes, halved

- ¼ cup basil, torn

- 2 tablespoons balsamic vinegar

Directions:

1. In a bowl, combine the zucchini noodles with salt, pepper and the oil, toss and leave aside for 10 minutes.

2. Add mozzarella, tomatoes, basil and vinegar, toss, divide between plates and serve as a side dish.

Nutrition:

Calories: 188

Fat: 6 Fiber: 8

Carbohydrates: 8

Protein: 6

Coconut Cauliflower Mash

Preparation Time: 10 minutes

Cooking Time: 10 minutes

Servings: 6

Ingredients:

- 2 cauliflower heads, florets separated

- 1/3 cup coconut cream

- 1/3 cup coconut milk

- 1 tablespoon chives, chopped

- A pinch of salt and black pepper

Directions:

1. Put some water in a pot, bring to a boil over medium-high heat, add cauliflower florets, cook them for 10 minutes, drain them well, mash using a potato masher and stir.

2. Add the cream, the coconut milk, salt, pepper and chives, stir well, divide between plates and serve as a side dish.

Nutrition: Calories: 200 Fat: 3 Fiber: 3 Carbohydrates: 12 Protein: 5

Parmesan Brussels Sprouts

Preparation Time: 10 minutes

Cooking Time: 30 minutes

Servings: 4

Ingredients:

- 1-pound Brussels sprouts, halved
- 1 teaspoon oregano, dried
- 1 tablespoon olive oil
- 3 garlic cloves, minced
- ½ teaspoon hot paprika
- A pinch of salt and black pepper
- 2 tablespoons keto ranch dressing
- 1 tablespoon parmesan, grated

Directions:

1. Spread the sprouts on a lined baking sheet, add oregano, oil, garlic, paprika, salt and pepper, toss, bake them in the oven at 425 degrees F for 30 minutes, add parmesan and keto ranch dressing, toss well, divide between plates and serve as a side dish.

Nutrition:

Calories: 222 Fat: 4

Fiber: 6

Carbohydrates: 12

Protein: 8

Fried Cauliflower Rice

Preparation Time: 10 minutes

Cooking Time: 15 minutes

Servings: 4

Ingredients:

- 1 tablespoon ghee, melted
- 1 small yellow onion, chopped
- 2 hot dogs, sliced
- 1 tablespoon avocado oil
- 1 garlic clove, minced
- 2 and ½ cups cauliflower rice, steamed
- 2 eggs, whisked
- 2 tablespoons coconut amino
- 2 scallions, sliced

Directions:

1. Heat up a pan with the ghee over medium-high heat, add onion, garlic and hot dogs, stir and cook for 5 minutes.

2. Add cauliflower rice and avocado oil, stir and cook for 5 minutes more.

3. Add the eggs, toss everything, and cook for 5 more minutes until the eggs are scrambled, add the amino and the scallions, toss, divide between plates and serve as a side dish.

Nutrition:
Calories: 200

Fat: 3

Fiber: 6

Carbohydrates: 12

Protein: 8

Cheesy Asparagus Dish

Preparation Time: 10 minutes

Cooking Time: 30 minutes

Servings: 6

Ingredients:

- 3 garlic cloves, minced

- ¾ cup coconut cream

- 2 pounds asparagus, trimmed

- 1 cup parmesan, grated

- A pinch of salt and black pepper

- 1 cup mozzarella, shredded

Directions:

1. In a baking dish, combine the asparagus with the garlic, cream, salt, pepper, mozzarella and top with the parmesan,

introduce in the oven and bake at 400 degrees F for 30 minutes.

2. Divide between plates and serve as a side dish.

Nutrition:

Calories: 200

Fat: 3

Fiber: 6

Carbohydrates: 12

Protein: 9

Roasted Cauliflower with Prosciutto, Capers, and Almonds.

Preparation Time: 10 minutes

Cooking Time: 25 minutes

Servings: 2

Ingredients:

- 12 ounces cauliflower florets (I get precut florets at Trader Joe's)
- 2 tablespoons leftover bacon grease, or olive oil
- Pink Himalayan salt
- Freshly ground black pepper
- 2 ounces sliced prosciutto, torn into small pieces
- ¼ cup slivered almonds
- 2 tablespoons capers

- 2 tablespoons grated Parmesan cheese

Directions:

1. Preheat the oven to 400 degrees F. Line a baking pan with a silicone baking mat or parchment paper.

2. Put the cauliflower florets in the prepared baking pan with the bacon grease, and season with pink Himalayan salt and pepper. Or if you are using olive oil instead, drizzle the cauliflower with olive oil and season with pink Himalayan salt and pepper.

3. Roast the cauliflower for 15 minutes.

4. Stir the cauliflower so all sides are coated with the bacon grease.

5. Distribute the prosciutto pieces in the pan. Then add the slivered almonds and capers. Stir to combine. Sprinkle the Parmesan cheese on top, and roast for 10 minutes more.

6. Divide between two plates, using a slotted spoon so you don't get excess grease in the plates, and serve.

Nutrition:

Calories: 288

Fat: 24g

Carbohydrates: 7

Fiber: 3

Protein: 14

Keto Jalapeno Poppers

Preparation Time: 10 minutes

Cooking Time: 20 minutes

Serving: 16

Ingredients

- 8 oz. cream cheese

- 1/2 cup shredded sharp cheddar cheese

- 1 tsp pink himalayan salt

- 1/2 tsp black pepper

- 8 jalapenos, halved, de-seeded

- 8 slices of bacon, cut in half

Directions:

1. Preheat stove to 375 degrees and line heating sheet with material paper.

2. Spot bacon cuts on paper towel-lined plate and microwave for 3 minutes. Put aside to somewhat cool.

3. In a medium bowl, include cream cheddar, destroyed sharp cheddar, salt, and pepper and microwave for 15 seconds. Mix together

4. Cautiously scoop cream cheddar blend into a plastic baggie

5. Wrap bacon cuts around jalapenos and stick with a toothpick.

6. Spot jalapenos on arranged heating sheet and prepare for 15 minutes.

7. Increment broiler warmth to cook and sear for 2-3 minutes, watching to guarantee cream cheddar doesn't consume.

8. Remove from broiler and permit cooling marginally before eating.

Nutrition

Calories 79

Fat 6.6g,

Carbs 2.1g,

Protein 8g

Barbecue Fat Balls

Preparation Time: 5 minutes

Cooking Time: 0 minutes

Serving: 6

Ingredients

- 4 ounces cream cheese

- 4 tbsp. bacon fat

- ½ tsp smoke flavor

- 2 drops stevia

- 1/8 tsp apple cider vinegar

- 1 tbsp. sweet smoked chili powder

Directions:

1. In a food processor, process all ingredients except chili powder until they form a smooth cream.

2. Scrap mixture and transfer into a small bowl, then refrigerate for 2 hours.

3. Form into 6 balls.

4. Sprinkle balls with chili powder, roll to coat well.

5. Serve.

Nutrition

Calories 146

Fat 14g

Carbs 1.5g

Protein 1.3g

Bacon-Wrapped Scallops

Preparation Time: 10 minutes

Cooking Time: 15 minute

Serving: 4

Ingredients

- 16 sea scallops

- 8 slices bacon

- 16 toothpicks

- olive oil for drizzling

- black pepper and kosher salt to taste

Directions:

1. Preheat broiler to 425°F.

2. Line a heating sheet with material paper. Put in a safe spot.

3. Envelop one scallop by using a half-reduce of bacon and comfortable with a toothpick.

4. Shower olive oil over every scallop and season with pepper and valid salt.

5. Orchestrate scallops in a solitary layer on a readied preparing sheet, giving every scallop some space to permit the bacon to clean.

6. Heat 12 to 15mins until scallop is sensitive and bacon is cooked through. Serve hot.

Nutrition
Calories 224

Fat 17g,

Carbs 2g,

Protein 12g

Low Carb Tortilla Pork Rind Wraps

Preparation Time: 10 minutes

Cooking Time: 30 minutes

Serving: 8 wraps

Ingredients

- 4 large eggs

- 3 ounces pork rinds

- ½ tsp garlic powder

- ¼ tsp ground cumin

- ¼ to ½ cup water

- avocado oil or coconut oil

Directions:

1. In a powerful blender or nourishment processor, consolidate the eggs, pork skins, garlic powder, and cumin. Mix until smooth and very much joined. Include 1/4

cup of the water and mix once more. On the off chance that the blend is extremely thick, keep on including water until it is the consistency of hotcake hitter.

2. Warmth a sparse 1/2 teaspoon of oil in an 8-inch nonstick skillet over medium-low warmth, include around 3 tablespoons of the hitter and utilize an elastic spatula to spread it meagerly over the base of the dish, nearly to the edges.

3. Cook for about a moment, until the base is starting to dark-colored.

4. Rehash with the rest of the player, adding oil to the skillet just as essential

5. Add more water to the player as required; it will thicken as it sits.

Nutrition
Calories 194, Fat 5.6g, Carbs 5.4g, Protein 9.7g

Avocado Chicken Salad

Preparation Time: 15 minutes

Cooking Time: 20 minutes

Serving: 3

Ingredients

- 3 avocados

- 1 lb. chicken (cooked in any way from this book)

- 1 medium tomato

- 1 onion

- 4 limes

- sea salt and fresh ground black pepper

Directions:

1. In an enormous bowl pound the avocados until smooth.

2. Include the chicken, onions, tomatoes, lime squeeze, salt, and pepper.

3. Blend well.

Nutrition

Calories 465,

Fat 38g,

Carbs 6.7g,

Protein 55g

Paleo-Italian Carpaccio

Preparation Time: 1hour 30 minutes

Cooking Time: 1 hour

Serving: 4

Ingredients

- 8 ounces of grass-fed, grass-finished filet mignon
- 1 bunch fresh organic Arugula
- 4 tsp truffle infused extra virgin olive oil
- 1 tsp unrefined sea salt
- freshly ground black pepper to taste

Directions:

1. Spot the meat in the cooler for around 2 hours. This will make it firm enough to cut with a sharp gourmet specialist's blade or with a meat slicer.

2. Cut meagerly and isolate the individual cuts laying them on 4 individual plates.

3. Organize the arugula over the meat, separating it similarly

4. Shower the oil on the plates, at that point sprinkle with salt and pepper

5. In the event that you are utilizing cheddar, mastermind the shaved parmesan on top

6. You can include extra naturally ground dark pepper to decorate the top.

7. Plates can be chilled in the icebox for 30 minutes before serving.

Nutrition Calories 437, Fat 28g, Carbs 4g, Protein 31g

Green Egg Scramble

Preparation Time: 10 minutes

Cooking Time: 5 minutes

Servings: 1

Ingredients:

- 2 eggs, whisked

- 25g (1oz) rocket (arugula) leaves

- 1 teaspoon chives, chopped

- 1 teaspoon fresh basil, chopped

- 1 teaspoon fresh parsley, chopped

- 1 tablespoon olive oil

Directions:

1. Mix the eggs together with the rocket (arugula) and herbs. Heat the oil in a frying pan and pour into the egg mixture. Gently stir until it's lightly scrambled. Season and serve.

Nutrition: Calories 250 Fat 5 Fiber 7 Carbs 8 Protein 11

Spiced Scramble

Preparation Time: 10 minutes

Cooking Time: 5 minutes

Servings: 1

Ingredients:

- 25g (1oz) kale, finely chopped

- 2 eggs

- 1 spring onion (scallion) finely chopped

- 1 teaspoon turmeric

- 1 tablespoon olive oil

- Sea salt

- Freshly ground black pepper

Directions:

1. Crack the eggs into a bowl. Add the turmeric and whisk them. Season with salt and pepper. Heat the oil in a frying pan, add the kale and spring onions (scallions) and cook until it has wilted. Pour in the beaten eggs and stir until eggs have scrambled together with the kale.

Nutrition:

Calories 259

Fat 3 Fiber 4

Carbs 3

Protein 9

Potato Bites

Preparation Time: 10 minutes

Cooking Time: 20 minutes

Servings: 3

Ingredients:

- 1 potato, sliced

- 2 bacon slices, already cooked and crumbled

- 1 small avocado, pitted and cubed

- Cooking spray

Directions:

1. Spread potato slices on a lined baking sheet, spray with cooking oil, introduce in the oven at 350 degrees F, bake for 20 minutes, arrange on a platter, top each

slice with avocado and crumbled bacon and serve as a snack.

Nutrition: Calories 180 Fat 4 Fiber 1 Carbs 8 Protein 6

Eggplant Salsa

Preparation Time: 10 minutes

Cooking Time: 10 minutes

Servings: 4

Ingredients:

- 1 and ½ cups tomatoes, chopped

- 3 cups eggplant, cubed

- A drizzle of olive oil

- 2 teaspoons capers

- 6 ounces' green olives, pitted and sliced

- 4 garlic cloves, minced

- 2 teaspoons balsamic vinegar

- 1 tablespoon basil, chopped

- Black pepper to the taste

Directions:

1. Heat a saucepan with the oil medium-high heat, add eggplant, stir and cook for 5 minutes.

2. Add tomatoes, capers, olives, garlic, vinegar, basil and black pepper, toss, cook for 5 minutes more, divide into small cups and serve cold.

Nutrition:

Calories 120

Fat 6

Fiber 5

Carbs 9

Protein 7

CONCLUSION

The things to watch out for when coming off keto are weight gain, bloating, more energy, and feeling hungry. The weight gain is nothing to freak out over; perhaps, you might not even gain any. It all depends on your diet, how your body processes carbs, and, of course, water weight. The length of your keto diet is a significant factor in how much weight you have lost, which is caused by the reduction of carbs. The bloating will occur because of the reintroduction of fibrous foods and your body getting used to digesting them again. The bloating van lasts for a few days to a few weeks. You will feel like you have more energy because carbs break down into glucose, which is the body's primary source of fuel. You may also notice better brain function and the ability to work out more.

Whether you have met your weight loss goals, your life changes, or you simply want to eat whatever you want again. You cannot just suddenly start consuming carbs again for it will shock your system. Have an idea of what you want to allow back into your consumption slowly. Be familiar with portion sizes and stick to that amount of carbs for the first few times you eat post-keto. Start with non-processed carbs like whole grain, beans, and fruits. Start slow and see how your body responds before resolving to add carbs one meal at a time.

The ketogenic diet is the ultimate tool you can use to plan your future. Can you picture being more involved, more productive and efficient, and more relaxed and energetic? That future is possible for you, and it does not have to be a complicated process to achieve that vision. You can choose right now to be healthier and slimmer and more fulfilled tomorrow. It is possible with the ketogenic diet. It does not just improve your physical health but your mental and emotional health as well. This diet improves your health holistically. Do not give up now as there will be quite a few days where you may think to yourself, "Why am I doing this?" and to answer that, simply focus on the goals you wish to achieve. A good diet enriched with all the proper nutrients is our best shot of achieving an active metabolism and efficient lifestyle. A lot of people think that the Keto diet is simply for people who are interested in losing weight. You will find that it is quite the opposite. There are intense keto diets where only 5 percent of the diet comes from carbs, 20 percent is from protein, and 75 percent is from fat. But even a modified version of this which involves consciously choosing foods low in carbohydrate and high in healthy fats is good enough. Thanks for reading this book. I hope it has provided you with enough insight to get you going. Don't put off getting started. The sooner you begin this diet, the sooner you'll start to notice an improvement in your health and well-being.

CPSIA information can be obtained
at www.ICGtesting.com
Printed in the USA
BVHW092304140621
609528BV00010B/1479